DREAMWORKS®

BEE MOVIE™

A GUIDE TO THE SWEET LIFE

DK

Contents

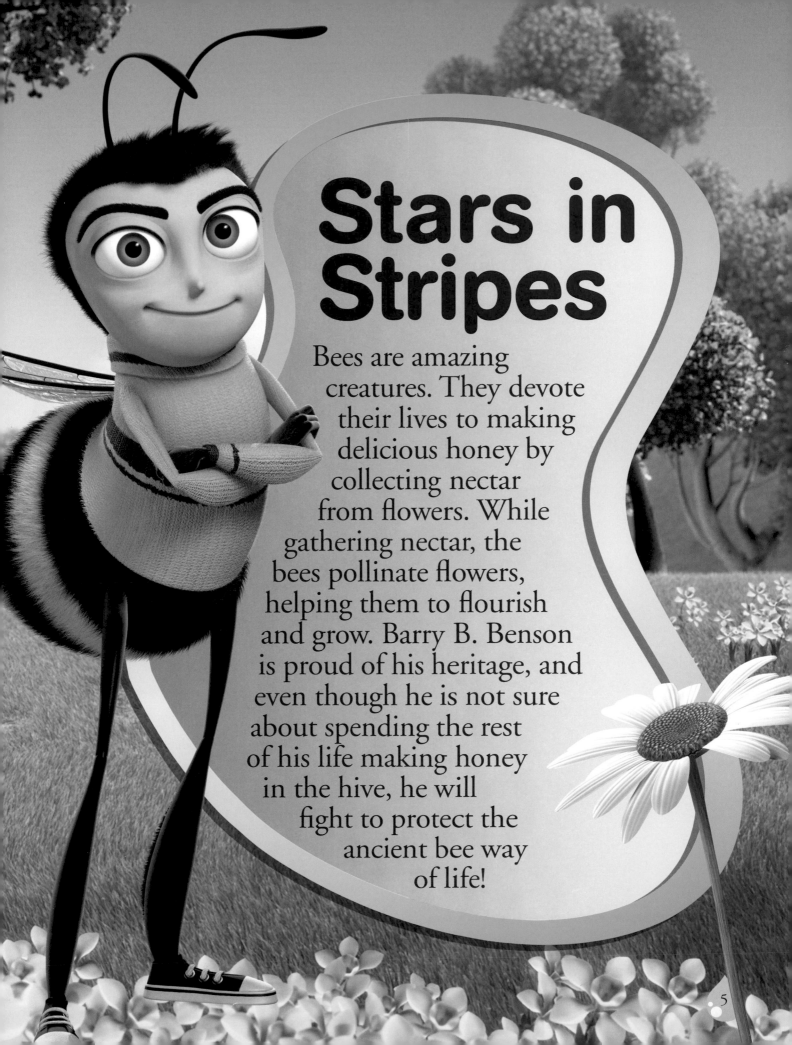

Stars in Stripes

Bees are amazing creatures. They devote their lives to making delicious honey by collecting nectar from flowers. While gathering nectar, the bees pollinate flowers, helping them to flourish and grow. Barry B. Benson is proud of his heritage, and even though he is not sure about spending the rest of his life making honey in the hive, he will fight to protect the ancient bee way of life!

Barry

Barry B. Benson is a bee who stands out from the swarm. Never one to conform to beehive behavior, this dude dares to think differently from other bees!

Antennae also receive phone calls and faxes

Streamline wings for hovering over flowers

High flier

Barry's certainly an ambitious bee, but he's going to have a mountain to climb if he wants to become President of the United States!

Barry's aiming higher than a life in the hive. Rather than bumbling about, Barry wants to spread his wings and do something different with his life.

Hidden stinger full of bee venom

Black and yellow sneakers to match his stripes

Travel bug

Barry is a bee who wants to fly off the beaten track. He wants to explore the outside world and is always curious to see what is around the next corner.

Bee meets girl

Despite it being against bee law to talk with humans, Barry speaks to Vanessa and gives her the surprise of her life!

When Vanessa saves Barry from being squashed by Ken, he's very grateful to her and soon the two become fascinated to hear about each other's world.

Laid-back attitude

Cool and confident, Barry knows how to turn on the charm. Witty and entertaining, this stripey guy is very good at making small talk with both humans and bees.

Adam

Adam Flayman is Barry's best buddy. From their college graduation to their first working day at Honex Industries, these guys stick together! Adam is fiercely loyal and fun-loving, but also very level-headed—Barry couldn't ask for a better friend.

Smart looking spectacles

Tie always neatly knotted

Fashionable Adam

Adam Flayman always dresses to impress. Usually wearing a smart tie and a sharp jacket, Adam likes to be at the cutting edge of fashion.

Adam is excited about working at Honex Industries and is certain he wants to work with honey. But when it comes to choosing which department to work in—he just can't decide!

Long stride, always going somewhere

Bug brothers
In the hive, male bees are known as drones. They don't actually do that much apart from mate with the Queen in order to produce eggs.

Bee reasonable

Adam is an insect with common sense. Whilst Barry wants to go flying outside the hive, Adam is always more down to earth. Often the voice of reason, Adam urges Barry to behave more like a bee and conform to life in the hive.

Hovering wings

Smart clothes remain unruffled

Adam has a sweet tooth. When he tries a crumb of human cake he's amazed at its great taste!

Plastic sandwich sword to replace sting

Adam finds it's a real pain in the butt when he stings Montgomery. Luckily Adam escapes death, but suffers temporary paralysis from the waist down. To aid his best buddy's recovery, Barry rushes to his bedside.

 # Vanessa

Caring and sweet-natured, beautiful Vanessa Bloome runs her own flower shop. She is independently minded and a loyal friend.

Let's bee friends

Vanessa likes to go with the flow. However, when she finds Barry can talk, it is just a little too weird. It's such a shock she pours coffee all over the floor!

Vanessa believes that all life has equal value. She acts quickly to save Barry when he is in danger of being swatted by her boyfriend, Ken.

Flowers from Vanessa's patio

Ken

Vanessa has questionable taste in boyfriends. She is currently dating Ken, a man who has some issues. Originally her tennis partner, it's no surprise that he made a bee-line for Vanessa! But how long will they stay together?

Wherever she might be, Vanessa is always well-presented and likes to wear bright colors. But she knows that appearances aren't everything—it's what's inside that counts.

Immaculately styled hair ......

Vanessa's favorite necklace ......

Vanessa's Shop

Vanessa runs a flower shop in New York City which is stocked full of flowers and plants. When you walk through the door your senses are bombarded with the sight of bright colorful petals and the smell of sweet scents. For bees like Barry, this place is heaven-sent!

Drawer full of gift labels

HELLO

Cash register

Colored tape to wrap bouquets

Say it with flowers

Be it fuchsias or freesias, carnations or chrysanthemums, you can buy a bouquet of your favorite flowers from Vanessa's store. Judging by what's on display, it seems Vanessa's favorite color is pink!

Fallen petals

Display bouquets
in pots

Vanessa loves working as a florist. Her parents wanted
her to become a doctor or a lawyer, but she was only
ever interested in flowers.

Ken again

Ken often comes
into the flower
shop to see Vanessa.
Making himself
feel at home, Ken
indulges in a
frozen yoghurt.

Larger
plants make
popular gifts

Vase for
single flower

Vanessa takes care to ensure that everything
is beautifully presented in her shop. She has a
natural talent for flower arranging!

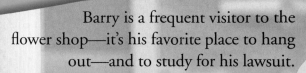

Barry is a frequent visitor to the
flower shop—it's his favorite place to hang
out—and to study for his lawsuit.

Barry's Parents

Martin and Janet Benson have worked very hard in the hive all their lives and these proud parents have high hopes for their son.

Green-tinted retro shades

Martin

Mr. Benson has been stirring honey all his adult life, a job he still finds fascinating. But it's now Barry's turn to cause a stir by not following in his father's footsteps.

Groovy brown and yellow blazer

Strong biceps from stirring honey

When they get a chance, the Bensons love to lounge around by their swimming pool on their own beehive balcony.

Beehive-style
hair do

Janet

Mrs. Benson is the
backbone of the
busy Benson family.
Whether baking
honey pancakes, or
ensuring Barry gets to
his graduation ceremony on
time, she makes sure everything
goes to plan. When it comes to
organization, Janet is queen bee!

Big sixties
sunglasses

Fashionable
yellow
polo-neck
top

Barry's parents are
very concerned by his
reluctance to commit
to a career in honey.
They soon start to
drone on about him
getting a proper job.

Martin and
Janet have had
a very happy and
successful marriage.
Ever since their
honeymoon, life
has been sweet!

Hive highness
Did you know in
any one hive there
is only one queen bee
who can actually
lay eggs?

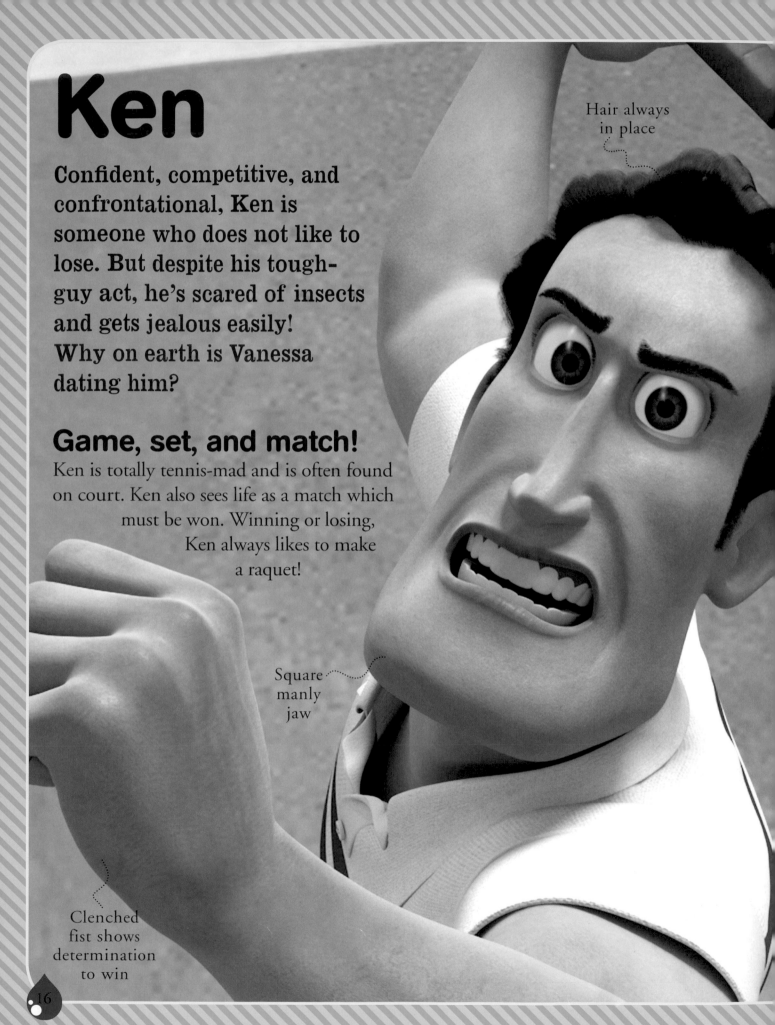

Ken

Confident, competitive, and confrontational, Ken is someone who does not like to lose. But despite his tough-guy act, he's scared of insects and gets jealous easily! Why on earth is Vanessa dating him?

Game, set, and match!

Ken is totally tennis-mad and is often found on court. Ken also sees life as a match which must be won. Winning or losing, Ken always likes to make a raquet!

Hair always in place

Square manly jaw

Clenched fist shows determination to win

Andy and Anna are two of Ken's closest friends, but he even gets into arguments with them. In fact the only thing they all agree on is that they don't like bees.

Ken is nearly as highly strung as his tennis raquet

Buzz off!
Some people are very nervous around bees because they have an allergy to them. Most people only have a mild reaction if they get stung, but some people can become very ill and may even die if they do not receive treatment. Luckily it is rare to be allergic to bees.

Hard sell
Ken's job is to sell artificial diamonds called Ziamoniques, but he can't even persuade his friends to buy any!

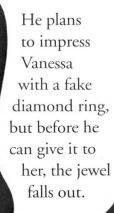

He plans to impress Vanessa with a fake diamond ring, but before he can give it to her, the jewel falls out.

Barry & Vanessa

Although Barry and Vanessa have not known each other for long, they really enjoy each other's company. Despite their difference in size and species, they soon become close friends.

Relaxed smile

Leaning comfortably

Beauty and the bee

Ever since she saved his life, Vanessa has been very protective of Barry. She is also fascinated to hear all about what it's like to be a bee.

Initially Barry feels close to Vanessa because she saved his life. However, as he gets to know her better he realizes they have more things in common. Not only do they both love flowers, but they are also both free spirits!

Vanessa and Barry spend a lot of time chatting over coffee and cake.

Bee tour

Vanessa helps Barry explore the human world by taking him down some of the streets of New York. Unfortunately, a passer by swats Barry!

In one of Barry's daydreams, he flies alongside Vanessa as she flies an Ultra Light plane, which is painted black and yellow like a bee!

Light streamlined wings

Wheels for easy take-off and landing

Yellow crash helmet for protection

Buzz words
Did you know that bees communicate with each other by dancing? The frequency of the dance and the angle of their body can indicate to other bees where there is food outside the hive.

Bee Life

What is it like to be a bee in the human world? Being so small and with so many people trying to swat them, there's a whole range of dangers they have to avoid. You would not believe how hard bee life can be!

The great explorer

When he's stuck in Vanessa's apartment, Barry feels like an intrepid explorer lost in a land of giants. He has to keep all his wits about him just to keep afloat! The hive might be boring at times, but at least it's safe.

Without realizing what glass is, Barry hits his nose on the window pane. Ouch!

Sugar cube makes a great raft

Barry's luck dips when he lands in some guacamole! Thankfully, sharp-eyed Ken acts in time to prevent Barry becoming someone's lunch.

Highly stung

Did you know that after stinging somebody, bees die soon afterwards? The stinger and the lower part of the bee's anatomy are torn apart from the bee's body. It's not much fun for the person being stung either.

Barry mistakes the light for the sun, and thinks he's flying out of the apartment. When he collides with the 75-watt bulb, he doesn't know what's hit him.

Book club

People are always using books or magazines as weapons to swat bees. The greater the number of pages the more dangerous. Barry once lost a cousin to a very thick fashion magazine.

The Beehive

Barry lives in New Hive City, a hive crammed full of very busy bees. Whether working for Honex Industries seven days a week, riding around in their bee cars, or waxing lyrical about honey on their apartment balconies, the residents always create a buzz of activity.

All the individual bee apartments are layered on top of each other. It's a high rise hive!

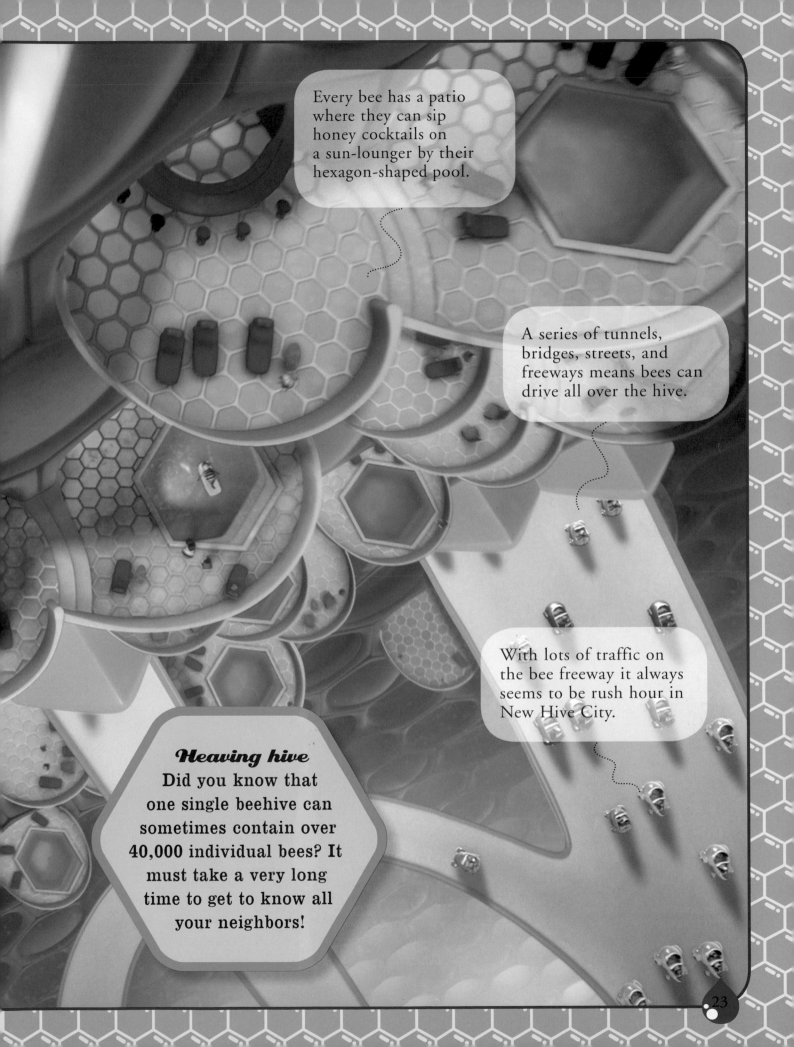

Every bee has a patio where they can sip honey cocktails on a sun-lounger by their hexagon-shaped pool.

A series of tunnels, bridges, streets, and freeways means bees can drive all over the hive.

With lots of traffic on the bee freeway it always seems to be rush hour in New Hive City.

Heaving hive
Did you know that one single beehive can sometimes contain over 40,000 individual bees? It must take a very long time to get to know all your neighbors!

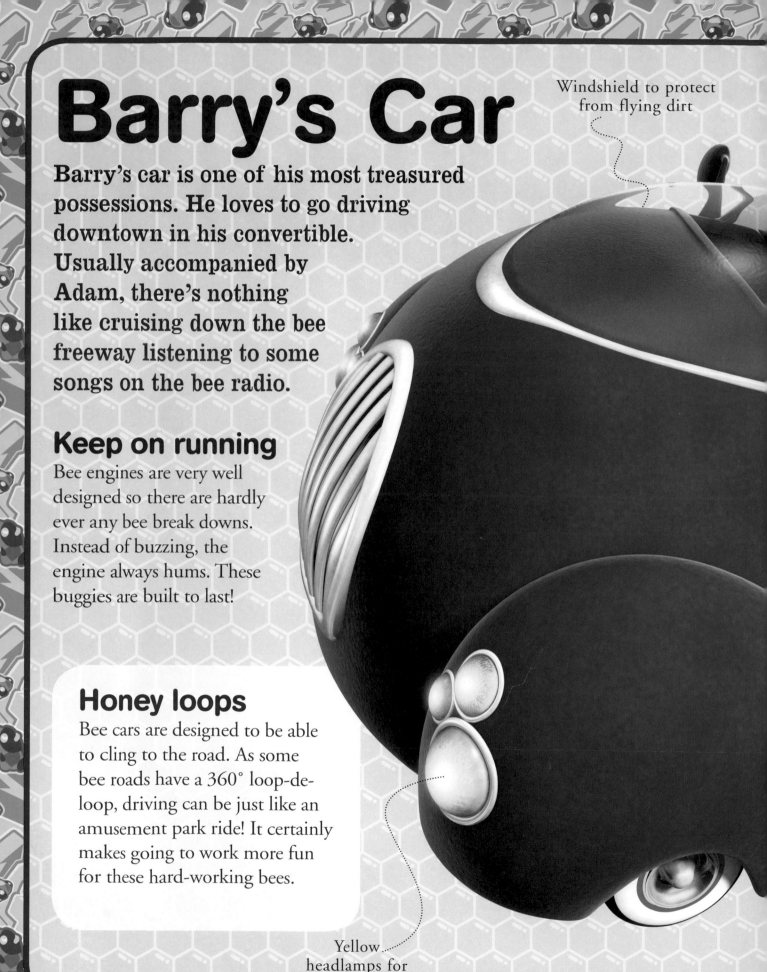

Barry's Car

Windshield to protect from flying dirt

Barry's car is one of his most treasured possessions. He loves to go driving downtown in his convertible. Usually accompanied by Adam, there's nothing like cruising down the bee freeway listening to some songs on the bee radio.

Keep on running

Bee engines are very well designed so there are hardly ever any bee break downs. Instead of buzzing, the engine always hums. These buggies are built to last!

Honey loops

Bee cars are designed to be able to cling to the road. As some bee roads have a 360° loop-de-loop, driving can be just like an amusement park ride! It certainly makes going to work more fun for these hard-working bees.

Yellow headlamps for dark tunnels

Barry gets a buzz being behind the wheel

Bee gone
Did you know that honey bees can fly a distance of up to 8.7 miles (14 kilometres) away from a hive? Although they only go that far on rare occasions, it's a very long way for a small bee!

Streamlined doors for improved aerodynamics

Impressive whitewall tires

It's a major surprise that Barry's convertible is actually red. It's about the only thing that he owns which isn't colored either black or yellow!

It's a gas!
Bee cars run on a special type of fuel. Rather than using diesel, they run on *beezel*, a fuel that's made out of honey. Beezel is totally ecologically friendly and leaves no pollution in the earth's atmosphere.

Pollen Jocks

The pollen jocks are a crack elite squadron of bees who go on deadly missions outside the hive to gather nectar from flowers. They are bee heroes!

Pollen helmet and goggles

Padded jump suit

On patrol

Bigger than most bees, and trained to face all sorts of dangers, the guys on pollen patrol mean business! Although initially meant as a joke, Barry swoops at a chance to fly with them outside the hive.

Barry has a taste for adventure but is about to go on a much bigger expedition than he bargained for. A trip on a tennis ball is not the usual way to earn your stripes.

The jocks need to be able to rely on each other 100%. Whether they are out finding flowers or flying in formation, these guys are the A-team of bees.

Anyone for tennis?

The pollen jocks see what they think is a field of flowers and go to investigate. The patches of yellow are actually balls on a tennis court.

Gun sight for taking aim

Suction cups

Barry gets stuck on a tennis ball and before he knows it, Ken has picked up the ball and hit it onto the court.

Clear barrel for collecting nectar

Honey money
Bees are very important to the world economy. They pollinate over 14 billion dollars worth of crops per year in the **US** alone.

RNF-issue boots

The pollen jocks use their special equipment to suck in nectar from the flowers. They take this back to the hive and empty it into huge tanks.

New York City

Both Barry and Vanessa live in New York City. From the grand Empire State Building to the famous Statue of Liberty, the Big Apple is one of the world's most beautiful and exciting cities.

Vanessa's view

Vanessa's apartment looks over beautiful Central Park, situated in the middle of Manhattan. Full of trees and flowers, the view from Vanessa's roof terrace makes it a great place to sit and watch the city go by.

High rise apartment block

Finders keepers

Human beings have been keeping bees for over 5000 years. It is possible that the original beekeepers came from ancient Egypt, as evidence of manmade beehives has been found there from about 2500 BC.

On the ball

New York is a big hit with Barry, but it's not without its dangers, especially with Ken on the tennis court! They say it's good to travel, but perhaps not at 60 miles per hour clinging to a ball!

Famous Manhattan skyline

New York can be a very busy and hectic place, making it a hazardous city for a small bee to visit. At least Barry can identify with the taxi cabs which are colored black and yellow.

Supermarket

Barry does not know what's in store when he visits the supermarket with Vanessa. Checking out the shelves, he is staggered to find jars of honey for sale. Barry is outraged that humans have been stealing honey from bees for years and making a tidy profit from all the bees' hard work.

Honey-roasted peanuts

Bugged

When he sees humans selling honey, Barry is livid that bees are the victims of such an enormous sting! He vows to get to the bottom of this outrageous injustice, explaining to Vanessa how honey is vital for bee's survival.

Whack attack!

Vanessa is stunned when Hector, a stock boy at the supermarket, tries to swat Barry with a rolled-up magazine. Vanessa values all life and doesn't appreciate it when her fellow humans try to hurt Barry.

Golden Blossom honey

Honey-flavored cookies

Cute Bee honey

Breakfast cereal with honey

Vanessa doesn't realize how her life is about to change when she goes to the supermarket for some groceries.

Honey Plot

When Barry vows to uncover the truth about honey and humans, he goes combing for clues. Going undercover, he soon finds himself hiding in the loading dock of the supermarket. The mission improbable has begun!

Camouflage

Show me the honey

Because his mission is top secret, Barry disguises his yellow stripes by coloring them in with a black magic marker. He also puts some stripes on his face. Despite his cunning disguise, Barry still looks very much like Barry!

Stealth pose

When Barry finds out the honey comes from Honey Farms, he chases the truck as it drives away through the city.

Boxes full of honey

Delivery

Taking stock

Barry observes Hector in the supermarket stockroom opening a box full of jars of the stolen honey. It is direct evidence of a secret anti-insect conspiracy! Now Barry is determined to find out where the honey comes from.

Honey spill

DELIVERY LIST
OPERATION SCHEDULE

When Barry confronts Hector they battle it out with a swordfight. Hector uses a pushpin to fight off Barry and his vicious sting. When Barry wins, Hector admits the honey comes from Honey Farms.

33

Insects

When Barry manages to hitch a ride on the Honey Farms truck, he finds life isn't easy for insects. Barry knows that the world is full of hazards and hardships, but traveling on the outside of a truck is even more dangerous for bugs!

Bug buddy

Barry meets Mooseblood, a mosquito who knows exactly how to survive on a truck windshield. He prevents Barry getting wiped out by telling him to play dead.

Goggles to wear when flying

Sharp proboscis to suck blood

Mooseblood Mosquito might suck blood, but he's no sucker. This guy knows what to do to stay alive. Because he gets swatted every time he tries to bite anyone, he's been forced to live by his wits. Even shunned by lady mosquitoes, Mooseblood is used to being a loner.

Powerful wings for quick getaways

Thick long

Hit and run

Some of the bugs on the truck don't make it. A ladybug on her way to Tacoma and a cricket clinging onto a radio aerial are some of the lucky ones who survive.

When the water bug witnesses Ken trying to squash Barry he declares he's not going to take sides. Is he a sensible insect or a cowardly creepy crawly?

Not taking sides

Long legs to aid take-off

Mooseblood decides to hitch a ride north to Alaska, where he's planning to drink some moose blood. Apparently it's the strongest blood around!

Media Frenzy

When Barry decides to take the human honey industry to court, the bee media start buzzing around, sensing a sensational story. Barry is suddenly thrust under the media spotlight and overnight he goes from a humble bee to the center of attention.

Scoop!

Whether making the headlines on the Hive at Five daily news, or appearing as the star guest on chat shows, Barry's 15 minutes of fame continues as the bee media swarms around him for another exclusive.

Wave to the viewers

Big smile for the cameras

Barry's life might be a hive of activity but he's still able to stay level-headed and put a lot of preparation into his case.

Trial by media

When Vanessa and Barry start court proceedings they never suspect it could be such a massive story. Soon human TV news crews, press, and paparazzi are descending on the courthouse creating a media circus.

News heavyweight Bob Bumble is the anchor on the Hive at Five TV news. Every evening Bob and his team get to the bottom of all the day's top stories, live from the hive.

SUPERIOR COURT
52 Chambers St.
New York, NY 10007

Pearly white teeth

Moustache immaculately trimmed

Trademark stripey suit

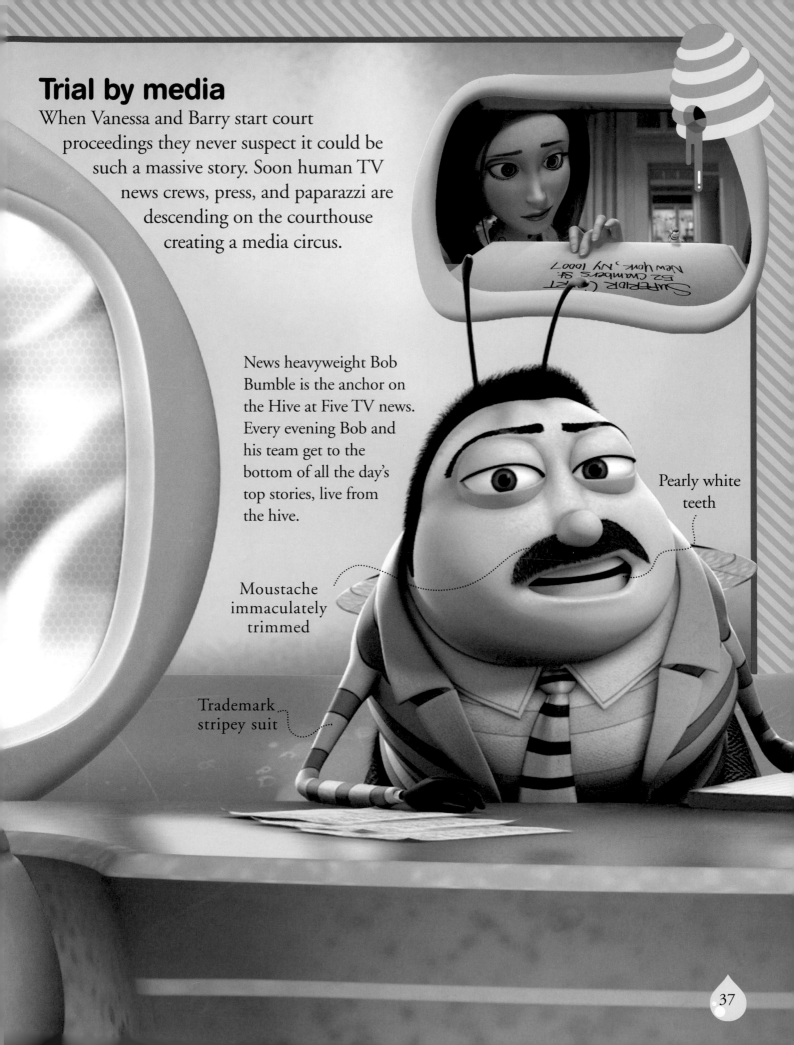

Court of Law

Determined to stop humans stealing honey, Barry—with Vanessa and Adam's help—takes on the might of the entire human honey industry in court.

Exhibit A—the bee smoker

Smoking gun

Barry and Vanessa's main evidence is a bee smoker, which is used to sedate bees. With proof that bees have been mistreated by humans, the defense are in the line of fire!

Vanessa demonstrates the bee smoker

If Barry can win, it is definitely going to be a victory for the little guys! In fact, the scale of the win will be unprecedented.

Montgomery P. Layton

Devious and determined, Montgomery P. Layton acts as the honey industry's defense. He will tell downright lies to discredit bees and picture them as stripey savages. When he tries to prove his point by provoking a bee to sting him, impulsive Adam falls for the trap.

As the court case continues, the 12 men and women of the jury hear the evidence of several witnesses. Those who testify include a film star who owns a brand of honey and an angry bear who hates bees.

Rest your case

Leading the defense team can be hungry work. At Vanessa's apartment Barry uses a doll's toy dinner set to eat his evening meal and raise a glass to the bee team.

Doll's fork

Pink plastic champagne glass

Half a pea

Plate the size of a button

The New Y

no.12212

In it for tl

Yesterday the notorious honey trial ended suddenly with a dramatic victory for the bees. Amongst chaotic scenes, chief prosecuting bee, Barry B. Benson was knocked to the ground, when he high-fived fellow prosecutor Vanessa Bloome.

The defense had been tipped to win for the duration of the trial. When Adam Flayman, a bee on the prosecution legal team, stung chief defense lawyer Layton P. Montgomery, the case was considered closed. However, the trial took a dramatic U-turn when the jury learned of the "smoking" method used to sedate bees. The judge ruled in favor of the bees just moments later.

The scales o

The win follows on only several weeks after it was discovered that bees can speak and freely converse with humans.

Jubilan

Last night t Benson's hi Today a fly

rk Telegram

$1

e Honey

e tip in favor of Barry B. Benson and the bees

enes in Benson's beehive

re spontaneous celebrations in Barry B.
h partying going on into the small hours.
y the Royal Nectar Force is planned, as well
the first in the entire history of bees.

Last night commentators were speculating what the victory will mean to the honey industry, with some predicting that all honey will be confiscated and returned to the bees.

Ken Attacks

Ken has a bee in his bonnet about the amount of time Barry is spending with Vanessa and starts to get jealous. Ken already dislikes insects, so when he finds Barry alone in Vanessa's bathroom he seeks his revenge.

Spray away

Ken attacks Barry with a rolled up magazine. When he misses, he grabs a can of floral air freshener to spray at Barry. What Ken doesn't realize is that bees love the smell of flowers!

Barry realizes he's met his match when Vanessa's bug-hating boyfriend lights the stream of gas from the air freshener so that it becomes a lethal flamethrower.

Determined look

Air

Air Freshener

Flower

Non-crease slacks

Second helpings

When Vanessa hears the commotion from her bathroom, she finds Ken about to hit Barry with a toilet brush! Rushing to Barry's rescue, Vanessa helps save him from Ken for a second time.

Even under attack, Barry's on a roll

There is chaos in the bathroom as clumsy Ken falls over into the shower. When he gets up, he sets the shower head to "lethal" and knocks Barry into the toilet with the water jet.

Flowerless World

Now that bees have won their honey back, they have so much surplus honey that they don't need to produce any more. The effects are dramatic. As flowers are no longer being pollinated, they soon start to fade and wilt away, with areas like Central Park become a barren wasteland.

Pond ducks have flown away

No meadow flowers

No visitors to the park

Shut down

Vanessa is saddened to see Central Park so empty and bare. She's also had to shut her flower shop because she has nothing to sell. The situation is very serious because soon there will be no more fruit and vegetables. This means there will be no food for anyone to eat.

Both Barry and Vanessa feel responsible for the terrible situation and wish they could turn back the clock. Getting out of this crisis is certainly not going to be a walk in the park!

Bare branches

Barry decides that he's going to be the bee to fix this mess. All it needs is a Plan B to get back all the flowers. Luckily a seed of an idea starts to grow in his mind.

Roof garden plants dying

Barry the Hero

Barry and Vanessa save the day when they manage to find the last flowers on earth at the Tournament of Roses parade in Pasadena. After flying them all the way back to New York, Barry soon mobilizes all the bees in the city to pollinate them. When flowers return to Central Park, it means Barry's plan has worked.

The blossoms are back

Meadow full of green grass again

Happy ending

Now the panic's over, it's lovely to have a picnic in Central Park. The sun is shining, the flowers are blooming again, and Barry and Vanessa have saved the day.

It's thirsty
work saving
the planet!

Hard work
A worker bee might
only make about a twelfth
of a teaspoon of honey
in their entire lifetime. It's
a lot of work to make a
full pot!

The bee's knees

With a little help from his friends, Barry
has managed to save the world from ecological
disaster. It's not a bad day's work for a small bee!
As well as being a hero to both bees and humans,
he's even made an honorary pollen jock.

Of course Barry enjoys the sweet smell
of success. However, he's modest about
his achievements and is still the same
bee that he's always been.

DK

London, New York, Munich,
Melbourne, and Delhi

Project Editor Heather Scott
Senior Designer Lisa Crowe
Brand Manager Robert Perry
Publishing Manager Simon Beecroft
Category Publisher Siobhan Williamson/Alex Allan
Production Julia Bovis

First published in the United States in 2007
by DK Publishing, 375 Hudson Street
New York, New York 10014

07 08 09 10 11 10 9 8 7 6 5 4 3 2 1
BD312—09/07

DK books are available at special discounts when
purchased in bulk for sales
promotions, premiums, fund-
raising, or educational use.
For details contact:
DK Publishing Special Markets
375 Hudson Street
New York, New York 10014
SpecialSales@dk.com

A catalog record for this book
is available from the Library
of Congress.
ISBN: 978-0-7566-3210-6

Color reproduction by
Media Development and
Printing Ltd, UK
Printed and bound by Lake
Book Manufacturing, USA

**Discover more at
www. dk.com**